SAYINGS WAR DEFINITIONS AGE
TIME HUMOR INSIGHT PETS
POLITICS IRISH RELIGION

Pocket POEMS *Anytime*

WGD

CALLWYN BOOKS USA

ABOUT THE BOOK/AUTHOR

Poems here spring from a mind pensive, light and free. Several sayings included might belong among your own. No lofting to high reaches. Life at the core is simple. Best we stay close.

WGD, new to the published world, considers work the important thing – not the writer's identity. He trusts you will find something here among the pages to gladden this purchase now, and if you carry *Pocket* POEMS with you, many times.

Copyright © 2013 Wm. G. Deckelman
CALLWYN BOOKS USA

CONTENTS

Humor	1
Beauty/Art	11
War	15
Dogs/Cats	21
Definitions	29
Politics	37
Sayings	45
Ireland/Irish	51
Love of Life/Philosophy	63
The Water/Hunt	69
Time	75
Age	81
Insight	91
Children/Education	107
Other	113
Religion	133

For Nellie and Henry

HUMOR
The final hour
On the final path
If I bring along something
The Lord will laugh

IN HELL
Asleep on the couch was her husband
The fire too hot for her bread
She shook him but all he answered
was GO? We just got here, he said

DOCTOR!
Pulse down
Pressure cool
Walking early mornings
Like an energy-fit fool
Watching diet
Dropping weight
Measuring spirits intake
What'ya want?
I'm strong as an ox
Look in my eyes
See the glow?
Am I taking the pills ...?
SO THAT'S WHAT YOU KNOW!

NIGHT

A bump upon the hardness of the house
Disturbs not people, but the mouse
Deserving respect as accorded all
Mice had no sin and didn't fall

Sounds affront little ears resting
Bring alertness at no time for testing
Startle what ought be in dream
Tempt to kitchen in hope of cream

Quiet is best at night for slumber
But there are exceptions to that number
Even a mouse at times goes about
When the cat scratches the door for out

May everyone here live in peace
And at night, bang quietly, if you please

EITHER OR

There are two choices in life:
Look in, or look out
If you're looking in all the time
Look out!

STIMULUS
If we gave you money
Would you spend or save?
Would you save the money we gave?

O, we like to spend
We hate to see money rot
But buy what?
Buy something we already got?

WORK
To be a spirit ...
And not need rest at all!
Work is fine
Till tiredness makes it toil

CHANGE
I see wrinkles, I see gray
I see eyes of a better day
Sitting over standing
Much more understanding
Changes
Have come my way

I see tripping over toys
(toys not really there)
My home's more user friendly
And takes less care

There's sleeping on the couch
Dinner table too
If only night had one more hour
And day lopped off a few

I see aspirations slipping
A lacking to be bold
O, it's more than I can stand
... All my friends are old!

MEDICAL CARE
If you're rushed when fishing
See a doctor
Otherwise
Keep fishing

GRAVESTONE
I had my will
I stood my ground
See?
I stand it still

HUNTING WE GO
A late fall day in a field I hunt
With me a dog once called runt
A deer in sight raised all our ears
I cocked the hammer but held my cheers
A slimy thing slipped hat to ears
The blast scared the deer, the dog ran away
The distance now empty, my spirit gone
I'd do better sleeping on a summer's lawn
What's an old hunter like me expect
With a gun-shy dog and a frog on his neck?

MORNING
Out the door to the black and cool
Foot falling foot like a lumbering fool
Mind alive as a roaming hog
Alone?
I'm like walking a dog

PICTURES
I painted things I thought I had seen
Sometimes what I saw
With vision poor
What I painted, wasn't there
But as I said
What I saw

STEPS IN EXISTENCE
Becoming aware of increasing life
Feeling how good its array
Hoping it lasts forever and ever
Working for riches each day

Lost in the cosmos
Shooting for the moon
Dying a billion years too soon

LIFE
The cat has nine lives
A man has nine innings
Then after
Can't get in with a ticket

A pretty woman
Has to have a good mouth
Watch yours

BIRTHDAY
Creation was not finished
Until October 9
When in among the airs of time
I burst forth my Irish line

How to know at such an age
That such a race of people
Fought with words, not guns
And prayed beneath a steeple

A lifetime later now
Looking cleanly at the lay
It was a world more peaceful
On my own entrance day

There are far too many warriors Arm-
chaired the worst
Had I to do it over
My first cry'd be a curse

I've lumbered over mountains
Crossed in ships the seas
Yes, listened to the gentle sounds
Of hummingbirds and bees

If peace is not a message
And only a word to say
I rue October 9
And may not be here to stay

RICH
Remember before tightening your grip
Tickets to wealth are always round trip

TECHNOLOGY
I'm using technology
It's working fine
Except when it doesn't
(I pay it no mind)
There's a hum to my work
I work with pride
Like a dog with three legs
Keeping the stride

HELLO!
Hate to come unannounced as we do
But passing the neighborhood through
Thought ...
Better be seen and not just heard
We're here for a minute
(an hour's third)
Don't re-arrange furniture
On your mind's lawn
I tell ya, we'll soon be gone
Just a blip and your radar's clean
We'll walk off
Like bugs in a dream

BEAUTY/ART

ART
Art is a muddy pool
Made white
For a moment
By a fish

Mournful song
Of joy yet to be
A dove in reverie
Upon a tree

REDWOODS
In the mist of quiet wood
Silence hummed, everywhere stood
Sunlight filters the scented air
The ground is needles soft as hair

See in wonder
Look without words
Heaven's entered
There were no doors

Persistent flower
In a rainy sky
Show your color
Show a moist eye

―――

Abstract art is like a preacher
Remote from the people

MARYLAND
A tapestry
a country road cuts through
If you're ever in heaven,
remember you knew

WAR

DYING SOLDIER
Nineteen, life at a draw
Hardly seen what I saw

WAR
Need the peace dove be as large as you
That you see peace in what you do
Who counsels war
As the only way forward?
Who leads the alarmed to death again?

NO MAN'S LAND
Descending through the war-borne air
Tranquil now but still absurd
Fluttering creature between shots
No one thinks to shoot a bird

Birds: close enough for study
Don't we see they know much more?
They witness man's eternal destruction
In vain attempts to even a score

How do birds avert this gloom?
How does a species opt for peace?
Our memories get an hour's room
Is the bigger brain wisdom's doom?

WAR
Show the faces of families at home
our bombs from the air would burn, entomb
Say once more the great necessity to rip this womb

1923
Lie there sunlit, trapped in grass
Our homes delight in music
Like no war ever was

THE LEADER
Standing apart, in little betterments which told his rank
He directed the men from lunch
And led them through a wood to clearing's edge
There – opposite – the enemy waited with cannon ... as plain as a Sunday drill field

In a charge no child would make,
They died to a man
Grasses blew as before,
little put upon by human necessities
It would be five hours till supper

THE ENEMY
You're bright, intelligent, smiling ...
Don't you understand, you have to be killed?

ARMED FORCE
Haste hurdles the javelin into air
Emotion & wisdom seem the same
Time brings thoughts slowly to earth
And we bargain back bodies from the grave

WAR, YOU SAY
Worse than dried fruit, burnt toast
It's the extrusion of life from thought
It's analysis by the stomach
It's abstract: like making love with
mathematics
It's men, unable to face anything but
yesterday, caving in
It's men with no backbone thinking war *is*
backbone
It's men not in it & far from it, not caring
It's insult a man judges he cannot sleep on,
venting martial anger to be felt equally by
his own countrymen
It's a no brainer; it has to be
And a reminder, it is, that the world still
needs honest to goodness ordinary saints!

GLORY
Glory's what others feel
Glory is not real

FEEBLE CAUSES

Blown fat like balloons
to catch every eye & heart
How we rush, tripping to the scene
... and "pop"!
That cause was yesterday's ...
Tragic, wrong, dead

But, in a cave, our hearts wait,
like bats
To fly out again, blind

DOGS/CATS

OUTSIDE
Gratitude at being alive –
Many things to explore
All that kept her from it
Was a door

MUFFIN
Speak, my treasured friend
Your silent mouth not try?
Words would fail your feeling
Your heart is in your eyes

CAT WALK
Majesty in majestic fur
More royal than the royals were

EYES
Warm flame blowing the chill
Aroma of fish, the cat standing still
All around smelling hot bread sweet
Alone in the thicket a wolf we might meet

CAT AT THE WINDOW

From next door this cat
Black, brown, white
Comes every day
That is, she might

Sits on the sill
Whether dirty or clean
She takes the world as is
I mean

The sun lights her fur
Glistens her moves
Licking a paw
A turn of the head

She'd rather be here
At this moment in time
But give her a minute
And she's gone

YOUTHFUL DOG
Run, my life, run ...
Breathe freshness
Feel the sun
Past thorny shrubs
Through brightened fields
Out to the edge of the sea
Believing in muscle
Trusting youth
Lifting, dreaming
Blown like a cloud

CAT
Little animal, lumbering slow
Head to the ground, does not know
She's upholding part
Of life on earth

———

The cat can't understand
No one understanding
Because the cat understands so well

PUPPY MUFFIN
Stumbling on her delight to be
In her run from where she was to me
Fluffy bundle, no holding her joy
Eyes to everything she saw

LITTLE MOUSES
Aroma of cookies in the stove
Filled each and every little nose
Mama Mouse said come closer here
Papa and little mouses' heads appear
And – wooof – the flame went strong and hot
Mousses pushed out, cookies or not

Never the cleanest on the street
They enjoy the cold
Because they felt the heat

Dogs teach us how to act
In a universe we need not understand
The learned deal in multiplicity
The wise keep dogs at hand

OUT A WINDOW
Black splendor
Shining cat
Careless if its charms be seen
A cat's reasons are its own
Where it is
Where it's been
She is seer
You are seen

THE CAT

Sometimes they carry within inside
The only importance of universe pride
Ignoring us, who look to be seen
Head down pondering
Not happy, not mean
The playful cat? Not this one now
Retreated in catdom, soul to ground
As well be a camel, hypo, horse
Till later arising a friend, of course

A NAME

Ears down, docile
Image of outgoing love
Knows no language
Hears meaning in sound
By shear interest understands

To get and give attention
Reason enough to live
Loyalty never questioned
Each breath a belief in life
At peace in recurring boredom

In the eyes' depth a hidden light
Can adventure explode behind eyes that bright?
Song of God?
Inspiration to man
Casually, we call it a dog

APKAR
In 1500s Norway, and you may guess, winter,
Apkar, my dog and I, have just come in -- a fire already going.
The hard day makes us strikingly tired: searching for a friend
and stumbling on a scene of war (for on yonder slope, we were
attacked and driven home before really done).
There will be a day – I don't know if you realize Apkar – when
both of us will be gone, no longer here. Yes, and still we gaze
into time, uncaring in our sleepy fatigue.
But you, Apkar, who appear not interested by your dull look, I
know down within you there is a burning love of life, and you
would fight – tired or not – to hold fast to it. Me the same.

We are strange. Others, yet to come, will take our place.
They will be strange: it is a world we don't understand. They
will talk as we (better than humans) because there is a
knowing beyond words, that humans, knowing the words,
miss. Good Apkar (fingers working behind his ears) I am
almost with God in your presence. And feel a closeness of
him by your breath ... even *see* him behind your eyes.
Later, smoke in the room of hewn timber grew irresistibly
hypnotic. They fell from thought to slumber. A day on
earth done.

DEFINITIONS

DEFT
A way to say without saying
And do with no deed done

THE OYSTER
Alive and well the oyster was
Inside the oyster shell
What a pity oysters live
Alone
Alone as hell

DEBATES
Is talk the last refuge of the lost?
And quarreling the last fight?

TEMPTATION
A web between seen and desire
Pass with peril!
A spider waits with devil eyes
An angel through her fingers cries

WAITING

An idle time, mind unemployed
Waiting for something, perhaps annoyed
Departure from living, a hole – a void

No hint of thought, empty head
The person in the person fled
Better sleep or better be dead?
My soul so humble it bled

HATE

Up from the dead, hovering the ground
Stumbled (self-taught) ahead on his way
Toward the enemy that did him slay

As if memory lasts through death to life
He reached to his belt, pulled out a knife
Ever it seems, once learned of hate
Dried in the bone, remedy too late

Old age even, always the same
If walk at all, walks he with Cain

BONUS
Something your humility built up
in the expression of others

TO BE
The face of thanks is our face
The face of giving his
A gift a prime delight
Wrapped in the mirror's *is*

TALK SHOWS
With words they shout the scare of truth
 What Power decides alone aloof
Endless paintings of scenes to come
Arousing dread in everyone

WISDOM
What we *will* wish
What we do not want now
What others cannot understand

DEMOCRACY
The uneasy balance:
Power people think they have
And the power of the powerful

SEX
Facing into facing face
Proxies of the powerful God
Spark, the touch of meeting clouds
Spasm electric, silence aloud

FRIEND
A friend is a friend
Who rose to defend
Us
When we were not there

GAMBLING
Drifting on tonic elixir
Into nefarious fog
Chance becomes the predictor
Loss tallies the score

THE MARKET
Who enters into the murky dark
Sees things astounding day
Dim shadows scare about the place
Only devils stay

TRUTH
Ugly remembrance
Humanity's proof
Humility graphically restored

STUDENTS
A route to simple
Not seldom sought
To see the new that's n'er been thought
Granted rarely to them that taught

CHIPMAN-Z
And now what mischief might I mount
Riding forth on a world unseen
To tamper some with facts it holds
So safe and clean!

DEMOCRACY
The poor man's dictatorship.
Under a dictator, we pray things
will get better. With democracy,
we vote. And eventually find
prayer more effective.

THE SUPERIOR MIND
continually misjudges the
capacity of lesser minds –
those by which he'll be
described best.

A DAYDREAM
Can be worth ten hours television
And might carry some prayer credit

POLITICS

THE ELECTION
I stormed no ramparts
Nor challenged any man to a duel
My heat was all words
I risked the name fool

MAKING
Money, they make worth what they say
But can words create jobs?
Night be made day?

BREAKING POINT
A nation stops
When those who built it die
And men can strip it, try
And those whose loyalty is outdated
watch

POLITICIAN
Brings forth a new idea
(as old as ancient Greece)
To thirsty ears forgetful
The tease to ease their grief

"So it can never happen again...."
Each time something bad happens
(or something embarrassing)
Congress holds hearings to fashion
laws "so it can never happen again."
But nature obeys only its own laws. All
that's happened will happen again – if
not the same way, dressed *creatively*.

KILLING IT TO SAVE IT
Politics headstrong enough to destroy the
engine of governance, yields to forces
standing by, who never did like democracy.

POLITICAL PLANS
Trapped in mystery
Battling things we think exist
Who dares cry victory
over reclaimable gifts?

POWER WE HAVE
A famous general
(Was it Patton?) said bravery
was holding out one more minute.
We carry patience on too short a fuse.
First, our assumptions may be wrong.
Second, our assumptions may be wrong.

Time eventually brings truth, or
opportunity to see difference – or
learn our first sight was not best.
Impatience hardens views, creates
wrong ones in others and postpones
a mature, accurate analysis.

There is great power in holding on,
thinking further. We have that power.

THE NATION
A nation is an accumulation of dreams
Each person's ...
Leaders seem not to know

DECISION

Armies always need sleep
Keep getting hungry
Fear dark night's creep
Need time their families write
Enshrining the decision to fight
For armies, like mountains, the
real mission is height

TROUBLES

Giving a problem to the smartest
may not a solution gain
Not so much for logic
as taint in the brain

FAULT

How do people govern their governors?
And the governors govern too?
And people be at fault
for what the governors do?

MOVEMENT
Across a field
Lead or led
I followed what
My heart said

Four times it changed
Before I crossed
My first intention
Truly lost

VALUES
When profit wars with wages
And money's more valuable than men
A question prays to heaven
Is righteousness expressed in yen?

Is valor all a myth?
Does courage run and hide?
Is love essentially personal?
In the nation, no pride?

CAPITOL
Hallowed white stones
Shining in day
Within, ever dark,
Amidst grins of decay

CHIVALRY
Men weasel and cave
Often and grave
In ordinary days
They fear to be brave

VALUES
Real ones have to be marbled
into our hours, day by day
To speak of what we *hold*
is like the sedentary person
who does not do exercise
but believes in it

THE NATION

There is no nation
It's a construct, a security blanket –
even for non-socialists
It fills the need of Big Mother
for the grown

QUIET SCOTSMAN

I saw a need
With time to act
But never did ...
I thought and didn't say the thing
And died afore the fact

SAYINGS

Suffer your friends

Vision is a perception
It is not total

———

Persist in duty beyond strength
Into a strength unknown

———

REFLECTION
Whether at work or play
Brain time is too dear
To listen all the words we hear

I AM
I see, therefore I am
And because I am, I think
of what I see

———

Reason is a tool available
It is not part of the machine itself

———

AWARE
Wisdom is not so much knowing facts
As guidance around the facts we know

JOAN
Glory is duty never fame
Steps you take end not in gain

WEALTH?
Only one question we seek of the dead:
How great their spirit, instead

GETTING
You get from others in every unconscious way
What you ask for
There is no justice that makes a lie true

COVENANT
Blood is power's written right to reign

SANITY
Sane are those
In whom sanity and emotion are distinct

———

Who brings more truth
Upon the scene
Is seen himself
A charlateen

ALONE
No scene same
Seen by one

———

SMART is something WISE forgot
WISE is something SMART is not

IRELAND/IRISH

SYMPATHY
Another Irish saint is borne
To heaven through a shroud of green
To heaven whence the Irish come
What a shortness in between

1916
A poet's war by poets brung
And poets on conclusion hung

BANTRY BAY
Lap of a gentle wave
Feel of a hand on the wood
Songful groan of the oars
Every man would fish if he could

Skies encompass the beauty
Of shores, islands, trees
Light illumines the softness
Adding blueness to the seas

What better hours spends a man
Daylight in old clothes
Down on the open water
The sea smells the sweetest rose

OF IRELAND

Whistling tunes as you walk the road
It's Irish speed for the journey's load
Taken aback by an upcoming fork?
Sit down a bit and pop the cork

Everyone wishes Irish or not
To hold that spirit Ireland's got
Swelling the chest, fresh air or not
Every day was made for laughter

1916 TIME OF ANGUISH

Poetry: a daring plan
Action time afoot the land
Would everyone show?
Would others rise?
What of breakfast the following day?

Must a poem *take* breath to give it life?
Do men die to see it read?
In my brain the words have life
Who takes them when I'm dead?

EREAN
Candle of life, the runner's task
Ask not the feet nor look back
Carry the seed, no matter the face
Onward the Irish race

IRELAND
O fresh spring-like beauty
slumbering isle in the sea
Open, ye clouds, open
That I rest my eyes on thee

SNAPSHOT
Voices, wind, rain
Soulful touchstones
What Ireland was
Before our time began

THE DAY

How ponders this priest
To a house not far walking?
The call, a custom duty of his kind
He, above the work & dirt of toil
A life of thought, prayer, things unseen
To bring to peasants what peasants' hands cannot
the sight of wonder even in their midst
an air of holy in their common life

White cottage door – out in front the family
Standing, dancing in fright
The widow's hand, unwashed, out to greet him
Her eyes, the only words her person spoke

A kindly man, his hair askew and blowing
Saw all the welcome due his calling's task
His palm touching faces, all three children
Calming slightly the throes of frenzied woe

Inside the stark, earth-floor fetid dimness
A man on straw, in quiet sleep can't do
The blessing to him slowly murmured low
A thumb to vacant forehead, rigid feet

The saddest day in life for these poor children
The earth alas had failed them once and good
And though the day be sunlit, dry and comely
A wetness soaked all vision as rain would

Father, who made all 'happened happen
Father went and left us all in pain
No more stories by flicker light of candle
No more donkey rides for us again

"Ma, you said the loss to you was greatest.
Can't God bring back da's life to us again?"

IRISH
Is it that the Irish are agreeable
Kind and generous?
Well, no, they are but not always
It's more a synthesis of being
A heady, humble, bright inventive grasp
Upon the world which takes the edge
from despair
Brings a sense of laughter back the air
And reminds the richest thing of earth
is friendship

THE HEAVENS OF MAYO
Mary, Mary, in a land without worry
How does your garden grow?
Does it wave in the breeze of passing bees?
Does it stand aloft, no care to rain?
Does it whisper with birds and little girls?
And dance when the air says dance?
And still be there when morning comes
To fill your window pane

IRISH FUNERAL

A load on the shoulder, the wood
is hard
Jostling hands snuggle the ear
Inside the box, a stone we bear

Birds alight, clouds disperse
Branches bend in gentleness

Eyes show minds of inward pause
Time has stopped a while

Carefree words, jokes, his laugh
The hope in life he showed and gave
Stilled, as we saunter down the path
Buried, before we reach the grave

NELLIE

Those who made her mad
On her wrath could sure depend
Behind their backs
Her Irish broke
Their goodness she'd defend

FIGHTING FANTASY
It was Finbar who broke from our weakening line
Ran without orders, out to the side
Up toward the heights the enemy held
Into the hail he drew now

"He's gone," a man yelled
"No, he's running again"
Out from the gulley, zigzagging his way
"On Finbar, lad" we cried
As gunners trained the most lavish fire

Finbar went down: he was hit and he lay
Silence all guns, the foe anxious to say
That crazy brave soldier was dead

His head rose – birth of surprise
He dragged one leg, wormed on his side
Aghast in wonder, the enemy froze
Watching Finbar and their positions close

Silence. Could this drama have more?
Then Finbar fired grenades restarting the war

He stood up!   All saw him, bad leg and all
Lumbered ahead in a continuing fall
Firing away, unconcerned about death
When a flash seemed to lift him up off the earth

We looked at each other, saw ourselves lifted too
Clouds all around, skies almost blue
The last thought of all, be they friend or foe
Was Finbar! ~ Finbar! Look at him go!

THE COTTAGE

The floor was dirt
Hands and mind as well inert
A hunting hound, afield aflung
A fox come home was all there was
A drinking man, his cares naught
This house, this home, his money bought
Its light, its dark, its cold, its warm
This house is where his life is gone

TRADITIONAL IRISH MUSIC

The sentimental feeling game
"Nostalgia" is my middle name
I love the music Ireland hates
I sing and strum to recreate
What never was, but I don't care
My world is make believe, oh yeah
My world is make believe

A CAT

Tommy grabbed the cat by its loose handle of fur-skin behind the head – black, shiny.

Stepping along to his fishing spot, he swung it captively all the way to a high place on the bank of the river Liffey.

"I got me a cat, a cat, a cat" he ran pole- over-the-shoulder, jumbled in his cadence.

But did Tommy know? He held a plan for the morning, an emerging light appetite for mice, a yearn to stare creatures (especially people) in the eye with superiority born of higher awareness, a healthy propensity to arch the back and twitch the tail (such that, if you knew the signals, you'd see what the cat was telling you); a soft-footer who considered the earth tender in all places touched, a progenic world of cats – in a dark place beneath the fur waiting to be born.

Tommy couldn't guess. He knew nothing of cats compared to his sister.

JESUS!
A knock on the door – dark and spooky
A hoary maid jumps at the sound
No second of thought afore takes the handle
swinging wide open the door

A pair of eyes meeting those of her own
In the black broken only by snow
Come in, wont ye, taste of our spirits
And the hulk moves through inside

Sit here by the fire, ye must be frozen
as her clasp goes after the brew
she hands him last year's, just from the
cellar *It's better by far than the new*

I ask was he wandering long in the snow
He stares me straight, two eyeballs say no
Then walking he's been, many days long
On the morning I'll hear words to his song

Hand of the hulk goes grabbing the glass
But his head slumps down
And that slump was his last

Wait till I tell the ladies at church
Those bitches of piety thick as the turf
They'll say it was Jesus, paying a call
Come bury him then; he lies in me hall

LOVE OF LIFE PHILOSOPHY

PHILOSOPHY is the eventual rumination after we discover life lasts 100 years and we are already_____!

The simplest things are best in the world
Look at the puppy curled on the rug
Sleeping daytime to make good the hours
Complete harmony, a garden of flowers

SPRING
Let foreign minions mesh in battle
And pirates seize their helpless prey
Let wolves chase down a bleating sheep
And hawks drive calm birds away

Every storm has its thunder
Every smart man falls to blunder
All that's wrong is here to stay
But spring comes anyway

Gold, art, things we cherish
Aren't worth so much if friendships perish
Lift the latch, push the pane
Smile again with spring

AUTUMN
Deciduous fall
Bright symbol of death
With gusto we burst to its air

BLACK UP
Night sky is for earthlings' wonder
Not lit by anyone
Who can count the hundreds blinking?
What it means, can any say?
Excitement hits the senses reeling
Two different worlds in a single day

THE WORLD GONE SPIRITUAL
You buy stuff without substance
Not seen as is
Everything's digital
Buried in a giz
For $2.99 the world's almost free
Smaller and smaller
Believe but no see

WAR
The look of a face
Feeling akin
No war with these faces ever again
How did it happen so much before?
We know not our neighbors next door

MOST NATURAL
Dying comes to flowers and trees
To flying birds and little bees
None are missed in this glorious plan
A winner replaced by an also ran

———

Leave no eyes undotted
Nor goods scattered o'er the moor
One box into the grave
One for posterity's store

MONDRAGON
Reading the will of de Mondragon
Shocked the year, 1565
All inheritors dead and gone
Were they for-warned?

Living men who read this now
Refuse to know they quickly pass
Don't see time slashing years by the hundreds
Ahead as in the past

FAME
Acclaim –how loud when I am dead?
Deaf these ears and eyes of mine
And others, burdened, do they have time?
Sighs, whys – any word?
Intra pulvis interred!

GRAINS
If we are grains of sand
On a wide long beach
Why just lie there?
Be a good grain!
Love the sky, the water!
Love the rest of the beach!

THE WATER/HUNT

PINEY POINT
Down the river where the tall pines grow
Expanse to the bay, Virginia shore low
The ghost, the spirit of ever-gone times
Revives myself in the sun

THE PENSIONER
Warm the bench, kind the wood
And there the blinding sea
Memories clash with the noise
I'm only part of the glare

TITANIC
Cries of the dying go quiet
Arms thrash the sea no more
Calm comes an even surface
The moon hides its face in a cloud

Boats hold still for a listen
Alert to vision of life
Waiting, the one task on earth
Alive, the cold feel of night

ON THE WATER
My line unschooled, yet grew taught
Reeling in a fish I caught
Moved my boat as the warden neared
Fishing and talk I always feared
A citation sure would make me late
Was the first uncooked I ever ate

SINGING BEACH
Hot to feet, the sand was soft
Sauntered low unto the sea
Sky made slabs of water bright
Crabs were feeding nonchalant
Lapping sound, expansive sight
Beach grass gawking like clowns might
A step made noise of sweet delight

UNION
Feathered hook by the fish seen
In a cold flowing mountain stream
Angler wading with morning hopes
Amid seclusion and sunlight

Each tree separate as fish or man
In unity because each is here
Overlooked higher by a grazing deer
A kingdom alive in peace

PINEY POINT
Point of pines, where are you?
A hundred years and you are gone?
Crusts and sand, trees and grass
What to stir the soul of a lass?
Music, dancing, all past!
Quiet moonlight hums in silence
Memories groan, but they last

Battered by waves
Blown by storm
Held existing
By this reed connecting
What I cannot see

PINEY POINT
The road's the same
Where it goes
But can't go where it did
Only small piles of brick and slab
Where joy once never hid

PINEY POINT
Do I see ships?
Sails?
The blue extends so far ...
Sight is like a restless dog
The mind becomes a star

TIME

Time opens the unimportance
of many things

HOW TIME PASSES
You think it's slow
Can't see it move
Do something big
Then look back years
It can't be that long
I remember it so ...
Time is the craziest, laziest
 ... fastest thing we know

RACE ACROSS THE DESERT
Starters flexed black silhouettes
Before the flash of early dawn
Running brave on hard cool sands
Dreams and power strong

Before the heat of ten o'clock
Before reptiles crept to rocks
Before the eagle dove on prey
A lagging loser fell that day

As runners ahead faded sight
The laggard lost his gallant fight
His record ruined by that plight
Yet beat the sun off the earth that night

SUMMER SLOW

Was the time long ago
When speed wasn't fast but rather slow
To think was half to dream, you know
Passing events, mysterious some
Day and night endless hum
Serenity beats no faster drum

Return such days?
Live natural life?
Abandon worry?
Forsake strife?
The world would think you odd
It might
Happen if you tried it right

PRESENT
Our eyes see it, it is not past
But the belt is moving
Reaching toward tomorrow

PAST
The gathering place everyone recognizes
It is large
And now a part of us

———

How long is now?
How long then?
And to what extent
Do we mean by when?

TIME
Quick the days disappear
And not all thoughts become history

TIME
Remember once and always hold
All is short though lengthy told
Life's warm groweth cold
Move! Or to death be sold

AGE

GOOD THOUGHT
In milky fog of morning
When bird sounds don't offend
Think of mending a friendship
With a half-broken friend

RISE
When you rise, expect a voice
Quietly hear it say
You, your life and earthly dreams
Are granted one more day

KNOWING
Takes a lifetime to learn
Still we die ignorant
So light up the fire and pause:
What to learn? what to do?
And what to begin to cause?

PERSON
Think of loved ones,
The historic, the great
Is it flesh you remember?
Or spirit you rate?

OLD AGE
How the limber look on life
No dream of getting gray
See the aged as always old
Proper, they look that way

Over years, knowledge comes
Seen as well as heard
The strangest thing in all the world
How that change occurred

CHANGE
Enough my life has filled the spaces
Behind the eyes that saw it all
Now I tread to other places
Where simpler things rise and fall

GOOD TIMES

I felt the crunch, my feet on the straw
The barn had a smell animals make
Wide and airy I sat with coffee
Remembering old days on the farm

There were no tractors; horses pulled the plow
There was no milker; *we* milked the cow
If something needed doing, we always knew how
If help were needed, neighbors came right now

All the world seemed wonderfully natural
Everyone worked like a family team
Life in the country was good for the soul
We must ever come back to that dream

SWIFTER
Lovers need few words spoken
Dogs go by sight and sound
Spirit moves unseen in air
Hitting ahead a smile's aware

EIGHTY SOME
I see my knees, existing in time
Existing in space, I feel my breath
Alive to the world, I touch my face

Alive I move, I touch my ear
I rise to see who else is here
I squeeze blood from out of time
I make days sing songs of mine
The noise of sweat, the muscle ache
My breath is no mistake

GETTING BACK
Strength's like bones
Wider than bones
Under the skin oozing out
Lying in bed, no test of steel
Venture abroad
Need you to heal

PASSING THE BUCK

Look no glory or roses thrown
When heirs converge upon your bones
On your carcass foretell their lives
A dead man needed for some to thrive

See your death as planted seed
Sprouting tall in others' greed
But what if you do exercise?
Possibly *delay demise*?

What might one see, if one tries?
Dancing atoms, stuff of lies
Within their heads
Straight through their eyes!

POSTERITY

Working for posterity
Pares gravity to the bone
Thinking of payment?
A grave of your own!

TEA
Skeletal features, heavy robes
Balancing the cup to his lip lobes
Tea of warmth, liquefy parch
Even the dead lust a trickle in March

Maiden of Death dressed to kill
Not smiling, not stern, strong face strong will
Watchful of birds, turns away dogs
Enter here but turtles and frogs

Motions last when movement stops
Forever quick in the mind at the top
Blowing grasses, bees' wings wave
Home in the meadow, home here save

WHERE?
Now upon the earth I am
Countless ones before and gone
Why be bored and feel forlorn?
I'm still here and hardly worn

AGE
I've seen 'em
hunched I've seen
'em bunched
At wheelchair corners in the hall
I've seen short and tall – fall
I've seen walkers, air box talkers
But don't see a one that looks like me

Sightless seers, earpiece hearers
Afright of mirrors
That aint me

Of all the things the Bible told
Of all the readings that I've read
Of all's been said, that I dread
I wouldn't want to get old

UNKNOWING
Disaster's dark black look of hope
Evil not so bad as thought
Blood flows, life goes on
Here at the worst ...
Am I blessed or cursed?

ALIVE!
It's nice to be young when you're old
Nice to be warm in the cold
Life's a surrounding thing
My song and yours I sing

The sun is not far, it's near
Its feel on the skin proves a friend
A pause is no period, no end
Life is a thing to lend

PASSING
Dark streets the wagon's way
To skeletal ones on silent watch
Living holds remote its time
End, a blessing come to help

AGELESS

Delightful the breeze of the scene
Talking's just a noise in fog
Enjoying the feel it gives
To be around friends, like a dog

How old would you be, Satchel said
If you didn't know how old you was
Wisdom is where it is found
With man, horse or hound

Existing's an ongoing flow
With people unknown and you know
Young do better than old
Age best judged, not told

Count me young, the stone read
(just like always he said)
Stick with the eager, the bright
Make no call till you get through the night

INSIGHT

A day is like no other day
If a day I think new thoughts

HOPE
What we seek
Looks different in the gain
Hope is hope
And hope will hope again

UNEXAMINED LIFE ...
The over-serious life
In between
Is the carefree harmonious life

THE SQUIRREL
Defiant of risky heights
Confidence judging distance right
Tempts cats; runs not fights
Be brave, forget might

When I was young I hopped to the air
When tired, I dreamed without care
These were things I did as a kid
And as a man ...
The same I did
Or so same it seemed
But the more I lived
The more and more
I dreamed

ENDLESS CHRISTMAS
Those who bear the cost
Of friendship
Sacrificing momentary whims
Show a world of distracted complexity
The fine order
That can be made of things

Like the blind
Looking without sight
We see not
Only ... we might

The blind see
What sight does not reveal
The honest handshake feel
What a spirit looks like

Master plans we lay
For life's most simplest things

TO BE
A man can find himself
Fighting windmills
That threaten the air
Or building fanciful structures
That aren't really there

SEEING SELF
Talk, my mirror, booster of pride
Look instead into people's eyes
Gift of all gifts, gift of God
Who looks this mirror
From the other side

HURT
Foul verbiage
Unseen means
Lows the spirit
In another being

Physical wrath
Less the hurt
Than touch a soul
Without merit

ALIVE
Hardly we're born
And is
Till someone reads
We was

SUCCESS
In efforts toward success
In looking to get ahead
Listen to the turtle voice:
There is no lasting treasure
Spring is our only measure

Being sick is the blessing
Of subdued worry
Uncluttered thinking
Gentle quiet
The world does not appreciate
Sickness or its wonders

A PASSING LIFE
The desert dries
Its rain
And becomes the desert
Again

LIFE
Death sneaks in
A little like dusk
Dark is darker
Sleep is trust

WINDOW OF OPPORTUNITY
In an ocean
On a raft
A ship is seen far away
Like a dog whose need is apparent
To the dog
Men pray

MARKET RESULTS
Worry's acids eat at hope
Dreams slip slimy away
Changes marked in prices and health
The dead are buried every day

WOMAN

Her face made to show us how she is
Those eyes – stars – and we the watching skies
We peer, but look at what we cannot fully see
Touch her beauty only with our breath
A spirit roams here free before us all

HAPPY MAN

Land of peace
Man of peace
Work for family
Not for wealth
Gain by truth
Not by stealth
Happy is life

News, glitter
No minute to flitter
No gamble make
Nor drinking take
Watch what you see
Listen with care
The world's a trick
Never forget ...
You are a happy man

Mirror, mirror on the wall
Tell thy tale before I sleep
For dreams enhance or take away
Here I find what's true

Dear one, I am but polished glass
Seek your image in the eyes of God
(The ones he uses in passersby)
They'll tell what I must hide

WISDOM
If we could be wise
We would
But how can we rise through
Clouds of feelings?
And to whom could we speak
If we did?

POWER
I was aware
But status kept me still
If my spirit now is sad
It's because
I didn't know the power I had

FOG
You cover the body
You leave the soul
And desperate men
Are restless at the sight

———

Doing things we can't do
Squeezes juice thought forbidden
Into a life we believed only belonged to others

———

TO SUFFER
Pain by pain known
Close as flesh touches bone
Vain to look to other eyes
Words lack a hundred tries

TRUTH
You make yourself a liar
Not when you listen to what's heard
Later, when you break your word

PROOF
He didn't know he died
They buried still his bones
Did he ever live?
What proof did he give?

TO BE
Do nothing fast that can be slow
Hasten the sun? Let time flow
Those loved, let them know
And you are entering Paradise

COVENANT
We only give to Caesar what is his
What is our own, we covet like a dog his bone
A bird her twig
A bear his just-caught fish
Take away loyalty, if you take away this

CONFRONTATION
Role-playing's first play

YEARNING
Clowned to fashion first and fore
Afraid her simple self to be
Stood upon the earth in awe
As love passed by – once more

TREASURE
Thrice the diver dove, deep at treasure sought
And thrice came up empty-handed – naught
In he went a fourth time, swimming deeper than before
But when he found the treasure ship
It was mirage instead he saw

Coming to the fifth time, the diver didn't dive
He said he needed no more treasure
Than to live and breathe alive

SENSE
You see smart faces
More and more
Outsmarting the good
That brains are for

WHAT'S WRITTEN
It's not reading's task
To finish every parcel
But cast off most ...
Study, ponder
Add some to your arsenal

PEOPLE
I like knowing people who know
what they're doing
People to count on
People to trust

And other people
Who don't seem to know much
Other than treat you the best
Truly they meet the test

DIMENSIONS OF SOUL
Laughing is its giddy skin
Frowns vanish from the mind
Seeing outward more than in
Fearing not be left behind

There is no time
No feeling pain
Rise to light
And light again

MARK
Shell on the beach
A treasure one life left

OLD PHOTOGRAPHS
Stopped in the passing hours
Still believing in time
Quick were the minutes of forebears
Slow as a pulse are mine

GOD
Leave scientists alone
They'll prove there's a God

Urge clergy speak to them
And see how close God is

WHAT IT TAKES
God never made a gear
Clutch or semiconductor
Soft, loose-hanging wet stuff
(inside)
Make possible a living fish

ALIVE WITH THE LOWLY
Little faces, wobble steps
Exploring in a world of content
Money worries could only harm
The lowly weave reason
With enchanted charm

CHILRDREN/ EDUCATION

Children home laughing with dogs
A passing warmth
Loneliness may someday steal

ON THE DEATH OF A YOUNG ONE
So the rest go on
We can eat, sleep; we can play
What does it mean to be alive?
What does it mean today?

GOOSE TALK
Heaven gives down many gifts
Food, clothes, my place to rest
I'm thankful for all I get
But in the air my mind is high
Higher than wings allow
I see magic in motion
And beauty in the sky
I love creation all the more
The more that hits my eye

ZIPLINES TO OBLIVION

Ziplines through life are facile options presented the young as ways to get rich, rich and famous, rich and powerful. Rich, of course, meaning to accumulate.

Question: Should the young be encouraged to fall for this? Even by wiser ones saying nothing? If lifetime shortness is not calculated – even considered – the essence of human existence is easily perverted.

The world is really a work problem. Within a short span, what is the best work we can do?

EDUCATION

How to school up modern kids?
Most parents not lifting the lids
Teachers find their teaching task
Full of housework – and *teaching asked!*

Thought is highest of our acts
Thought is motion's greatest task

BEING SMART

There is always someone who seems smarter. Sometimes a guy gets mad because you don't catch on quick. The guy sees the difference in speed and rubs it in – either nastily or politely. But you get the point. And maybe you feel bad. Being smart is one thing. In life there are many. Being funny, for instance. People like people who make them laugh, more than people showing how smart they are.

Being kind is another. The world loves kind people. Because when you need kindness, you're probably in trouble; you can't figure something out. At that point you're ready for someone to help without showing off. That's being kind. The world is in great need of such people. There simply are not enough. And if you are kind, you will go over big, almost every day.

"Fast" is often confused with "smart." Fast people often do not keep trying. They quit if they can't do a thing right away. Sometimes slower ones work longer on things – staying on the job till they discover how it can work, or work better. Persistence is what all great inventors had.

Edison used to say he knew 900 ways a thing wouldn't work (because he already tried them). But things like the light bulb are here today because Edison persisted after many failures.

If the gap between smart people and the rest of us is so big ... why haven't the world's problems all been solved? Maybe the difference is not so great. Maybe problems require more than quickness.

There is room in this world for everybody willing to persist – to try, and try again. Like Edison.

OTHER

SOUND THE WHISTLE
Speak, though it takes the job you hold
Money loses value when it buys your soul

The panting dog has this to say
Lifting each breath of day
Life is heavy, but easy to weigh

Heavy hangs the breath and blood
Living days summer long
Lazy as a drifting fog
My match is that panting dog

GROUNDED (WWI)
Dreading war had ever come again
Our lives were after all the same
Listen to the patter o'r the trenches
When the firing stops, we all enjoy rain

LOVE

Far, far on a mountain hill
Where evergreens stand like soldiers still
The air carries memories, times once when
My love was here, the hour did not end

While eyes see, while feet are free
As mornings continue into evening mystery
My wish is that we did not part
Living is both natural and art

Love – Does it ever escape the heart?

DISTINCTIONS

Is there a distinction in naming days
and people living in them?
Together, as if they WERE together –
or maybe the same?

WALL STREETERS OF WWI
A simple leap to fame was the ambulance corps
But as oft happens in war
Death, not glory, lay in store

HERE, WHERE
The ancients wonder how people can live who
always look down
Missing the night array
that fixes our height
Giving HERE a new notion
All the universe in motion

NELLIE
Maybe one day she decided to be her full self
At the same time giving herself totally away
I don't know
Maybe it didn't happen in a day

The stories are fading now
Intact till she finally lay down
Funny, personal, times of old
Names and faces of all she told

COURAGE

It's an easy move to brave acclaim
Bravery and brave not the same
The higher call is harder met
When wisdom reins, nothing gets wet

Aggressive love the toughest denial
The bravest advance, the highest trial
Only the strong run toward this hurdle
Every toad in the world turns turtle

NELLIE

I was a girl at play in a yard
I had a dog named Babes
A big one, I loved
And he loved me
There was a fence and tree
My father worked at the hospital
My mother once worked there too
I was little, new in the world
Forever and ever ... like you

THE TRIP

From childhood's dream we walk
Through black streams where dangers lurk
Past happy days by sadness touched
Into dark heavens filled with light

IMPORTANT

Important things cut through routine
Character, will, love: these impress
We see plainly there was time – plenty time
Whether life was many days or one

DAY WORK

Cold fog brights north's roaring coast
A rubber-clad fisherman black to his boat
Sore of muscle, dim neath brow
A poor dripping catch from the infinite cow

Warmth and fireside tease the brain
The question is ever to sea again
Many a loss comes risking the ruff
A farmer's life not so tough

Talk to the sea, speak to the land
Listen to both and understand
The blood of one and the blood in me
Only mixes with life on the sea

IF EVER

If ever a cloud peeks open a ray
If ever a sudden kindness comes
If ever a dim world has something to say
Grab it
Carry it in your burdened heart
Blaze it from your eyes!

CAPITOL HILL
Sitting in the 1930s
In the tiny front yard of 202 E street
On a long wooden bench
Inside the fence
Looking over it (me through it)
Into a blackened street-light distance
Returning always to the drug store's near neon
Glaring gently, giving character to city life

Coolness was in relation to summer's heat
(The sidewalk remembered and would tell if we
touched it with bare feet)
My uncle, father, mother, sister and granny
Spoke things that floated in the lights
There was peace in the land
Together was life

GLORY
Rivers acknowledge no heroes
Battles had a life of their own
Deeds are writ in words
Words that corrupt the stone

INSIGHT
Between snippets of news
Thoughts unexpressed
Erupt sudden insights
Which pass with the next

HOPE
And so we watch
In the antechamber of nonchalance
After all, this is not the second war
There were many -- we lost count
What does hope of peace amount?

THE WAR IS DEAD
Stare no more grieving into clouds
Those who died are resting
The world's alive
Let eyes and ears heed
Be sober
There are mouths to feed

AFGHANISTAN
Down dead, in flowing clothes
Garment piles puff the earth
Does valor live? Or is it gone?
What of coffee next morn?
Who bears the load with a man not there?
Had I less bravery, less wanton flair ....
But birds fall every day

LAND
Grab the land
Fight for yours
Ever more holdings
But don't forget wars
Wherein good title
Changes to spoil
Correcting the fiction
Of owning at all

AFGHANISTAN
An inkling of light in the sky
Fades black
In a wide-open eye
Down, dumb, dead
The cause read
Expires in the head
In stillness lie soft stones

ROYALTY
Who knows the mind of a king?
Who sees thoughts in his eyes?
Who knows what evil they bring?
Who hears the song of surprise?

CAPTIVE
Worse than death, at least by five
In this tomb I lay alive

AFGHAN WAR VS. PEOPLE IN AFRICA
Huddled in hunger
Famine on the tongue
Against war they vie
For a place in our eye:
Less cost
More living
"No die"

PEOPLES' POLITICAL COMFORT ZONE
Who will lead us?
TRICKERS
When do we want them?
NOW!

CONFLICT
Would all wars' causes be clear
And the aftermath shown as well
There's no glory shooting for heaven
And find yourself in hell

ECONOMIC PLAN
When all the earth is acting tranquil
And no one's hassled or over worked
When all have time to laugh and talk
Maybe all, as well, will have work

A LADY'S HAVING
I didn't know from sunshine rain
The meaning the word ... gain
Unless the love of all the rest
And like a bird to build a nest

IQ
Nay to intelligence raw in the package
Beware it might read labels instead
Of finding what's true in existence around us
Capacity's sparkle can blink out dead

GRATITUDE
Motion, the heart of living science
Sees ever the same world looking new
Dawn brings existence fresh upon us
Rejoice in the breeze of motion's view

THE WOMAN
This old one, frail, wrinkled in the skin
Walks the streets phantom of her past
Memory holds glories of her girl days
When all the world was happy at her sight

None's flesh was faced quite so fairly
Her moves made magic in your view
Being near was truly heaven's blessing
As in those years many of us knew

She jerks an arm as would someone waving
To those who may see her on the street
And ups a finger on the moment mixing
Pixie with her curious ancient bleat

God keep her from a hell here/hereafter
May peace from others flow into her soul

JOHN KENNEDY
Young, brilliant in his turn away from arms
Surprising friends, but also men of greed
Who saw no wisdom in his move
And fearing peace, saw war the need
[In reference to JFK's speech at American University
shortly before his death, wherein he proposed a brave,
insightful chance for peace.]

UN SPEECH
Break a piece of truth? Crash!
It smashes on the floor
Laughter!
The world likes fiction more

EXISTING
Summers's laden load upon breathing
Makes thought too heavy for the brain
The future hangs shadows there before me
Distance is the truest thing of all

WAITING
Anything but wasteful
You plan ahead waiting
You're in control waiting
Ask forgiveness waiting
An idea comes waiting
You think of others waiting
(yes, you pray waiting)
You become both humble
and masterful

[For Mary Feeley]
COTTAGE MY MAYO COTTAGE
Neath the light of low-hung clouds
Fog floats in
Hiding playfully all it can
Lifting and laying, as a painter might
Saying No
To any connection with the world
Here is enough – right here!

POTOMAC FIELDS

As the coinless by their bootstraps rose
Many young men ran to fame
Pathways for the old not closed
If knees don't knock, legs go lame

The nation's a sold out bleacher
Catcalls, claps, cheers
For he who ventures late
With victory in his ear

The difference, only spirit
Ballooning up the will
To make it cross the finish line
Faint legs deaf to shrill

THE ART OF INTERRUPTION

Completion can be an obsession, obliterating good ideas (by a put-off tactic) a drive to first finish reading. Brilliant thoughts are lost – maybe forever. All in the name of saving time, being efficient. Better to stop at once, record the idea. Then decide what's more important: continue reading or develop the thought. Life is a search for ideas. We stop when we catch one. Like a tiger changing course. Like the vaulting eagle.

CHORES

When you're lifting the latch and looking to see
If the chores you left were done by me
When you examine the trash and the yard out back
---You'll be happy to know, I did that!

The letter to Rose, shine pots on the stove
Daisy been fed? Is the fence painted red?
---You'll be happy to know I did that!

Water the lawn, pull out some weeds
Fix the barn door or whatever it needs
Stretch the carpet, bang a few tacks
---You'll be happy to know I did that!

If you got so much done, you deserve having fun
Get a good book, find a nook
Where thoughts take you, there only look
---You'll be happy to know I found a good book. Speak softly, Mom: there's a fish on my hook!

VALENTINE
Time is measured many ways
Hours, weeks, days
All fail the truest test:
Each breath
Yours be mixed so much with mirth
You cannot decipher heaven from earth

ONWARD
I pull my wagon
Bounce cobblestone and clay
Mission drives me forward
To another rare puzzle named day

———

Here and gone in the time of a smile
And like a smile goes on beyond
The deed kindly done

VAN GOGH
How can it be so as is?
How can day follow day?
Bright, dark, flight of the lark
Death has its own curious way

... I heard a knock, but none was there
I climbed aloft ... without seeing
My sight was good, I was full aware
All I looked at ... stared

May Christmas delight you
The new year invite you
To days that like you
A life all charm

RELIGION

MYSELF YOURSELF
Never look to government to do your religion for you. Evangelization is always personal.

DIFFERENT AND SAME

In all the ways it disappoints
Troubles ever rising
Pain of the past: an unseen weight
Life is still surprising

Days never dreamed in childhood
Days that last on end
Ways to keep on going
Prayer to God might send

Prayer need not be formal
Nor wrapped in words too tight
A heart sends silent signals
Fast as speed of light

Those who pray and those who don't
Are not so easy told
Prayer of a non-praying person
From the heart, might be bold

Those who curse and use God's name
Irreverent though it seem
Are really crying out (in vain?)
For relief they need

Someone'll surely help them
See it's prayers they say
Tame an angry outburst
Maybe save their day

LOST WAY
Ancient critters crawl the ruins
Inward hopes flicker the past
Someone light a bush or candle
Is true God gone the earth at last?

The Christian life: feeble cold
Sparks no spirit, less yours take hold
And breathes forth air like sun-lit gold
A face – yours – love made bold

Thankful you planets
Keep speed and path
Heavens of wonder
Chaos is dead
Children of Adam
By a star led

God is motion
Soft, formless, alive

TO THE COMPLACENT CHRISTIAN
Leave no one's suffering, hunger, need
Nor stand you by and watch them bleed

TO WHERE
In a cosmos with no up or down
"to the side" is something we say
There is no vector of rational choice
Except follow Christ each day

———

We Catholics are carriers
We *possess* the faith
It does not animate
Nor program our day

GO
The length of life, a carried notion
May be likened to the span of the Mass
At a point in both, we truly swoon
"Missa est" is all too soon

MAKING
Create with the Creator
The whole expression of a face
Beam another sun on earth
Splash quotidian air with mirth

ANNIVERSARY
Hard to believe ten years is past
Did we do enough?
Did we think enough?

BRIEFING AT MASS
Our battle's not with guns
Here, among loved ones
Don't do what makes you sad
Grow lines in your face
That express the glad
Our battle is not with guns

FAITH
Think faith as a possession
Your first one
If you have a lot
Give some away

REAL OR FRAUD?
Belief is so trivial, so strikingly false?
Recurring events prove an equal remorse

Find life in exuberance
Protect it forever

HOLD ON
Gone is our faith ... unless something happens
Dead is the church ... without me
Silly to make it perfunctory
Grand when it's all it can be

With culture confused and erratic
Entertainment taking chunks of our lives
There's no clear difference from Pagans
The hope we all hoped has died

Walking the vague lanes of earthlings
Rushed, tired, unimpressed
There's one thing out there refreshing
Faith, back to life, before death

AYE
Star above a woodland tree
Be a special star for me
Be the Christmas star
That lights the tree that's me

FUNERAL
Look, see what lies before the crowd
An Irish sprite? A sleeping cloud?
A shopworn maid? A frightened child?

A willing helper when sleep was due
A fiercer friend you never knew

Not all took time to know her well
And now who comes offering praise?

But listen ... hear *her* speak:
"Let an Irish lady be
Do not with words this deaf one smote
You're yet to save yourselves! Unquote"

HEY, GAMBOLING GAMBLERS ...
A major problem now in the West is the tendency to
lay aside Christianity, the belief system that
infused our thinking with so much truth (science)
about life and nature. In these troubled times it
seems a good gamble to return to this generous
faith for many reasons, including selfish ones.

Solving the most unsolvable problems may await
return of this guidance system.

All roads lead to Rome (the city)
All thoughts stop at God

———

Lord, how could you see this dark bird
Flutter to a branch of this particular tree?
"Knowing, seeing and hearing all's heard
With your eyes I saw this bird"

MEDIEVAL CHURCH
Are Christian teachings superstition?
Are moderns smart and fully aware?
Ponder your inner self and worries
The stress and danger there

The Church teaches beginning and end
From the number 100, deduct your age
And see your life descend

FEARLESS MAN

Muscle galore one bullet kills
Brave talk's hallow as a gust of wind
Try serving the truth on prejudiced plates
Doing time in the cells of unjust states

The stature of a fearless man ...
We've seen them once
Will we see them again?

EULOGY, TOM DUDDY

This man was bigger than life. And unless
you stood next to him, it was so. His
presence loomed large in the mind
without a cubit added to his stature.
His voice – which had an easy volume –
boomed with authority, and at the same
time, his charm showed he was on
our side ... though he might change the
direction in which we headed.
Tom had only to look at you to call you
friend. This is an uncommon man
we're blessed with. He will not slip
easily from us, but go on, part of the
consciousness of what being a
Hibernian might mean.

PRAY FOR PEACE
And for Christ's sake
Act peaceful

FUNERAL OF NELLIE McCRORY
Can artist paint, or writer put down
The sights and sounds in that blessed
Sunlit enclosure?

A beautiful child
Gone loose from the pews
Climbing playfully the red stairs
Next into the arms of his mother
Dark hair against flaxen
Two faces, unafraid, hiding nothing
As they gazed and sang
Over a congregation in awe

And the dead one, Nellie, chattering
The handles of her coffin almost
As she sobbed, perhaps,
that death could be so grand

Then, spider-web delicate
Sounds coming further away
(near the organ) where a mind
Made suddenly whole
Formed union with God, Nellie
And with us all
Let it be a memory, if it is not a dream
Her silent, lip-moving prayers finally
Wrought something sensually substantial
And this, faith tells, is only the beginning

CHRISTMAS FUNERAL – 1989

Those filaments of love and hate, in there among the genes which make easy the ways a person is ... causing a specific name to call up the specter of wrath, gentleness, efficiency, patience, attractiveness, presence – the possibility that the world can operate, after all, on some underlying mystery of love.

But spirits exist mixed among matter, and matter (the hard stuff) outlasts them. These spirits dart – hummingbirds in the wind – off to places of their own, leaving us become what we will, in the haze and sunlight of short existence.

And so, Nellie McCrory, little girl, housewife, mother ... and in time lying here, trapped among the throng gathered to pay her honor – in public – before God.

Winter had come. Her springs were at last gone. But off somewhere, she is totally occupied in a now that does not elapse. And, we, yet ensnared in the webs of time can only pause, only envy.

WHY AN ECONOMY

Making money is a rule of viability – not in itself a goal. Our enterprises must look to their social purpose among the people. Profit – in the sense where workers are not a part is a dangerous, anti-social path.

Profit exclusive to the few must be protested, even boycotted, listening to no pipe dream which turns only into smoke for the rest.

As Pope Benedict XVI said, long before becoming pope: *without ethical foundation, market economies collapse.*

So much for what a holy man might know, what religion teaches about real life, and what sinners choose in avoiding education – because their desires have reached the high elevation of greed.

TALK WITH NELLIE

We talked at night in that room
I at the table
She in her darkened bed
Light through the door lit my head

I thought more often
But sometimes things I said
And, if awake, she answered
Softly back
The pauses long and easy
Much like conversation with the dead

As though we both had passed
And in some heaven
Where talk is measured by different rule
Our utterance spaced between clouds
Not rapid
Not slow
Not loud

SMILING JOHN

How do we speak of existence
Except in events that fall
He was refused space in the stall
(amiable man, Irish as Paddy's pig
yet so smelly as swine might wince)
Refused by the good lady, wife of Ard Ri,
leader of the Hibernians
She would not sniff what pigs shunned
And did not move when John approached
He could not get in the pew

It hurt us all, though we knew the cause
Poor John later died
And to much applause:
The church filled every pew
This spirit in our midst withdrew
Left us
With sweetened air
But gone the smile we loved and knew
And soon the lady tight on the bench
Herself struck dead
Her husband even, Ard Ri true
Dead – the three we knew
Died with them the hurts many felt
And felt by them

To live is pain among joy
John, come back to church with us
Sweet blossoms in our nostrils thrust

Beam your face upon the crowd
Your presence is a manger scene
Open air, breezes clean
Friendship, peace ...
Forgive us, John

CREATION
Every cat and creature
Looking what was done
For him, for her
For everyone

Requiem

Painted Curtain
So perfect we don't see
And fear or fail to lift
Who doubts their vision?

DECEASED:
The moon was lit
The canopy filled with stars
I awake to life
In a continuum of space and time
Thought not I to say thanks
For I considered myself part of all
I did not know my race began
And its destiny to fall
I had a brain
And one thing knowing
Thought it all

Then turned my gaze to earth
To distraction, indeed, mirth
I sought riches
Assumed timelessness ...
And now the second fall:
My parting from it all
I hope this musing here is close
Hidden from the priest and most

PRIEST:
Was he wise? Did he see matter as immaterial? Did he know form was image? Money a trick? Did he mistake getting ahead? Fall for saving and hard work? Did he realize one can never be rich – long?

DECEASED:
Breathing free
Steps wobbly
Against the wall
Had been so strong
Now the fall

A feel all through me:
Strange the warning
Sign to the wise
Death in disguise

Life starts ending
Dark descending
The call comes first
Inside the eyes

PRIEST:
Covet the earth
Grab an image
Hold to mist
Become the heir

CHOIR:
Body, words, go lofting
A pebble splashes sound
Hopes beneath the water sink
As chase rides after hound

You had minutes to laugh and work
Days to become best friend
Go now into time and space
Your face to others lend

PRIEST:
In short, was his interest greed (against a clock of fantastic speed)? Or generosity – giving – in tune with the Lord?
I'll not keep you stunned in eulogy
Aware how easily moderns are bored.
But burying an earthling
embraced of the creed
I speak brief words of common need
Arriving is simple; life looks long
The ending ends before we finish the song

Drop this down, now become earth again
Of dust made and into dust begin
And you here living, hold tight your grin
For all us go where the other has been
(from the grave looking back, most lives sin?)
Pray then all, as clocks tick day
To see material in enlightened way
(Hands and feet formless clay)

DECEASED:
My soul lies bare before the Lord
My sins are strewn about my feet
I know the weakness that I am
I know the commandments I failed to keep

PRIEST:
Amen

ABOUT THE BOOK/AUTHOR

Poems here spring from a mind pensive, light and free. Several sayings included might belong among your own. No lofting to high reaches. Life at the core is simple. Best we stay close.

WGD, new to the published world, considers work the important thing – not the writer's identity.   He trusts you will find something here among the pages to gladden this purchase now, and if you carry *Pocket* POEMS with you, many times.

www.ingramcontent.com/pod-product-compliance
Lightning Source LLC
Chambersburg PA
CBHW061326040426
42444CB00011B/2794